Johnny Morris's
BABY ANIMALS

Johnny Morris's
BABY
ANIMALS

Sundial

Endpapers: The baby giant tortoise has a long way to go before reaching the size of his mother.

Half-title: A young puma making his presence felt.

Title: This is a baby Asian elephant who will probably be put to work at hauling logs when he is grown up.

Contents: This one's lovely white coat will soon be replaced by a dark grey one, as he is a young grey seal.

**First published in 1981 by
Octopus Books Ltd
59 Grosvenor Street London W1**

© 1981 Hennerwood Publications Limited

ISBN 0 906320 54 2

Produced by Mandarin Publishers Ltd
22a Westlands Road Quarry Bay Hong Kong

Printed in Hong Kong

CONTENTS

INTRODUCTION

This book is about young animals and their parents. No doubt you will already have noticed how very determined these parents are to protect and rear as many of their children as possible. When your cat has kittens in your home, she chooses a nice snug place where the kittens will be comfortable and safe. She doesn't have to protect them, because she knows that she can trust you and everyone in your house to help her. But a wild cat is quite another matter. A wild cat with kittens is a very fierce animal indeed and so, of course, are many other wild animals.

There are other animals who cannot defend their young by fighting. They use other methods. They hide their babies. A deer has her fawn where there is plenty of cover, in the form of long grass, bushes and trees. The little fawn lies very still, while the mother goes away to find food. Like many little animals that hide, he is born with a coat that is lightly dappled, so that he's cleverly camouflaged, which means he matches and blends in with his background. You can walk within a few steps of a young fawn and not see it. Hiding is a very good way of protecting young animals. Foxes and rabbits hide in holes in the ground, lots of birds hide in trees or choose tall cliffs, where they are not hidden but cannot be got at.

In all these animals there is a strong instinct to preserve their young. Parent and child are very close together. However, it doesn't always happen like that. As you know, the cuckoo lays her egg in someone else's nest and leaves it for others to bring up. Then there are many reptiles and insects that lay hundreds of eggs and just leave them to hatch out on their own. They never see their offspring. We find this a bit strange since we are usually very closely linked to our parents. But the reptile that lays hundreds of eggs and leaves them, knows that her young will be able to fend for themselves up to a point. Many will perish but a few will become adults.

When you and I were very little we could not even walk about properly until we were nearly two years old and yet a baby horse — a foal — will make a brave try at a gallop only a few hours after it is born. So, however parents behave towards their young, you may be certain that their actions are designed to ensure that some young will survive and live to produce more young.

Johnny Morris

GRASSLANDS
and
DESERTS

The grasslands and even the deserts of the world are capable of supporting a great variety of wild animals. It is quite surprising to us to watch a rhinoceros eating a chunk of bush that we would only use to light a fire. Yet the rhino is able to convert rough bits of bush into a couple of tons of rhinoceros and there are many antelope that can exist on what we might call a tangle of old blackberry bush. However, there are others that need something a little more tender and they graze the grasslands. And where there are grazers you may be sure to find the ones that hunt and eat them.

RHINOCEROS (previous page) The little one in the picture is a very healthy and tough animal but the future for him is not a very cheerful one. He will not come to any harm or be injured by other animals except perhaps wild hunting dogs. He will always find enough food from trees and bushes, such as leaves and stalks, to keep him fit and lively. He will never roam too far away from the water because, like all the other black rhinoceroses, he does love to dabble in the water and wallow in the mud. So he should lead a happy life like a long, long seaside holiday. But the hard truth is that when he gets older and grows two big horns like his mother there, the chances are that he will be killed. He will be killed by hunters simply because they want those horns of his. They want those horns because in certain parts of the world it is believed that those horns, when ground down, provide a powerful medicine. So powerful and valuable is this so-called medicine that men are prepared to slaughter rhinoceroses without caring one little bit about whether there will be any rhinoceroses left in a few years time.

However, with a bit of luck, perhaps this little black rhinoceros may survive. He's not really black but a dark grey and in any case he will take on the colour of the mud he rolls in. He will be a roly poly mud colour. He will have a very keen sense of smell but will not be able to see very well. He will also become rather irritable and charge at anything he doesn't like the smell of, so you would be wise to keep out of his path. He will be a magnificent prehistoric type creature. Wish him luck.

BABOON (below) I wonder if the little fellow in the picture will one day be the boss of his troop. It's a job to say, because at the moment he looks a skinny little thing, doesn't he? But with a bit of luck he'll grow as big as the adult baboon in the picture. At the moment though he has to rely on his mother for transport. When he was very tiny he clung to her chest as she moved about but now he's almost big enough to ride on her back like a little jockey.

Baboons are very intelligent monkeys. They live in Africa and move about in fairly open country. They can climb trees when they want to but they generally stay on the ground. They travel around in troops and a ragged bunch of old tramps they look too. But in fact they are highly organized. There is a leader, who has helpers and they place themselves around the outside of the troop with the females and their young in the middle. If they are attacked, then the females make for the safety of the trees while the tough guys deal with whoever is causing trouble. And they are tough guys. They have got some pretty fearful teeth and they will not give up without a tremendous battle. The ones who try to catch them are the leopard and the lion but when they take on the baboons they know they have got some job on their hands. People have been known to make pets of baboons and some farmers in South Africa have used them as sheep dogs. But the smartest baboon of all was the one that was trained by a railway signalman to work his signal box. Do you think that British Rail would take on this little baboon as a trainee?

CHEETAH (above) I suppose everyone knows that this animal is the fastest land mammal. It can't go very fast for very long but when it makes its tremendous spurt, it can stretch its great gallop to 120 kilometres (75 miles) an hour. This little cheetah, like all cats that feed on flesh, must learn how to hunt, by first stalking a gazelle or antelope and then pouncing. It's a job to say just where these cheetahs are living. It could be Africa or it could be India. They have a very large range. It is often said that a cheetah is more like a dog than a cat. Well to start with, it can't climb trees, it's got very long legs, something like a greyhound and its claws are like dogs' claws rather than cats' claws. A cat can draw its claws back into its paw and stick them out when it wants to hook something. Dogs cannot do this, neither can cheetahs.

Sometimes in India, little cheetahs like this were captured live and taken to a Maharajah's palace, where they were tamed and trained. They were trained to hunt and catch animals for us. In the same way that we once trained falcons to hunt birds for us, so they used cheetahs to hunt animals. They even made hoods to cover their eyes just as we did for falcons. Then the cheetahs were taken out into the country where gazelles and antelope were quietly grazing. Now wild animals learned long ago to take fright when they saw the figure of a walking man. The legs going left, right, left, right. But wild animals do not seem to be too worried by the sight of motor cars or of a donkey and cart. Therefore the cheetahs and their handlers were put in a cart, so that they could get close to the antelope. Then the hoods were taken off and the cheetahs in one short burst were on top of the antelope. I sometimes wonder if a cheetah's eyes water when he runs so fast. Well, there seem to be two lovely tear stains down the sides of both the mother's and the baby's nose.

GIRAFFE This is as nice a picture as you could wish to see of a family of giraffes. Many babies when they are born don't look a bit like their parents. This generally applies to mothers who have to hide away in burrows or dens to have their babies. Baby rabbits and mice and lots of young birds are bald, not at all attractive and not a bit like their mum and dad. They eventually get like them of course but from the moment a baby giraffe struggles to its feet in the first hour or so of its life, it is a perfect miniature of its mother.

Like the gnu and the zebra, it must be able to run as soon as possible. These little miniatures were about one and a half metres (five and a half feet) tall when they were born and at six months will have grown over one metre (four feet) more. Fully grown they will probably be anything from four and a half to five and a half metres (16 to 18 feet) tall, just the right height for browsing amongst the tree tops. Giraffes are beautifully adapted to eat the things that other browsers cannot reach and it is really extraordinary that such delicate looking animals with such fine faces and long curling tongues can deal with the horrible coarse leaves and branches of the acacia trees.

Most animals leave giraffes alone. It is assumed they are just too big and too difficult a shape to deal with properly. There are stories of lions attacking giraffes and there are stories of lions getting killed by giraffes for they have a terrible back leg kick. They also have a high stamping front leg kick that is very dangerous. Yet despite their size they are ever so quiet, they don't make a noise.

LION (above) For a long, long time this animal has been known as the King of the Beasts and King of the Jungle. When you think of some of the kings of the past, the lion fully deserves his titles. He just sits about most of the day doing nothing at all. He doesn't have to do anything much. When he feels a bit peckish he and his lioness wives will gang up, go out and kill an antelope or a zebra or a wildebeeste or whatever happens to be handy. That could be their breakfast, lunch, tea and dinner for several days. So they sit in the shade and watch the antelope, zebra and wildebeeste working very hard eating grass all day long. They are herbivores or grass eaters. The lions eat them — they are carnivores or meat eaters.

Most lions live in Africa and they live together in large families. A family is known as a pride. A pride of lions because, I suppose, they look so proud. Like kings and queens. There may be about twenty lions in a pride. They are mostly mothers and children of various ages with one big father lion. He is the boss. A mother lion can have up to five cubs. When they are born they are quite helpless and very wobbly on their little legs. Mother never leaves them. Either Dad or Auntie Flo will bring her food from time to time. Then the cubs start playing. They play amongst themselves, they play with their mum, they play with Auntie Flo and their cousins. Play all day. They are really

playing at hunting and killing things. Just pretend hunting. Because if you are not a good hunter you are going to be quite hungry at times. Very soon their mother will take them out on little practice hunting trips. It may be in open country or it may be in fairly thick bush country.

NYALA (right) Hello, there's someone over there with a camera. The young male nyala is just a bit suspicious and so is the heron paddling about there. But mother and the baby nyala are quite happy to go on drinking.

The nyala is a most beautiful antelope and is a specialized bushbuck. As you can see it needs a drink now and again, in fact it never goes very far away from water. You can tell that the young one is a male because its horns are just beginning to grow and only the males have horns. There are many antelopes that have the same features as the nyala, that is the white stripes on the flanks and the strangely placed dots on the face and parts of the body. These three are probably having their evening drink, during the day they would be taking it easy in the bushes and feeding a little. The nyala is quite a timid animal and has to be very watchful of the leopard, because the leopard would have little trouble in dealing with the young nyala. But father is another matter and will not give in without quite a fight, as some leopards find to their cost.

DINGO (below) Right, now which one of these chubby puppies would you like to have? That is the trouble when you are choosing a puppy: unless you know the breed, you can never be sure what it will grow into. You can choose a dear little bundle of fluff and in a couple of years time you have a dog as big as a donkey. Well, if you choose one from this lot, it would grow into a pretty big dog and it would be a wild dog—a dingo. The dingoes live in Australia and they can be tamed but they are inclined to be a bit on the snappy side. Dingoes hunt very much as wolves hunt, in a pack, and they chase the animals they want and tire them out. As they live in Australia, they chase kangaroos and very often sheep. So they are not at all popular with sheep farmers and they are shot on sight.

It was thought that the dingo was a true wild dog. Later it was discovered that it was probably a domestic dog which had gone wild and produced its own particular size, shape and colour. After all, it is not uncommon for stray dogs to gang up and prowl about together and get up to all sorts of mischief. So in time, there could be a uniform type of dog emerging from a pack of strays. From the evidence that has been collected by archaeologists, it seems the dog was introduced into Australia in pre-historic times. So the ancestors of these wild little dingoes were well-behaved, tamed and quite civilized.

GREY KANGAROO (right) This mother and baby live in Australia and are marsupials. Marsupial is not too difficult a word—it simply means that the animal referred to has a pouch. The kangaroo is probably the best known marsupial of them all and there are about two hundred species of marsupials in the world. The little kangaroo when he is born is very, very little indeed. Not more than two and a half

centimetres (an inch) long and it is something of a miracle that he finds his way into his mother's pouch. Once inside the pouch he finds the very thing that will keep him alive and kicking—a nipple with a good supply of milk. There he suckles and grows and after about eight months he's big enough to come out and graze with all the other kangaroos, but he still returns to the pouch for the next few months. He

has to behave himself of course as the big boss kangaroo keeps an eye on him and everyone else in the mob to make sure there is no nonsense.

Kangaroos have been hunted in Australia because they were eating the grass that farmers wanted for their sheep. However, it is not all that easy to catch up with a kangaroo. It can leap along much faster than a horse can gallop, it can easily clear bushes two to two and a half metres (seven or eight feet) high and it almost certainly holds the record for the long jump, someone has measured a jump of 13 metres (44 feet). It's astonishing that a little creature that starts life just under three centimetres (about an inch) long will in quite a short time be able to jump over nine metres (30 feet).

CAMEL (left) The desert is not a very comfortable place in which to live. It is extremely hot during the day and quite cold at night. This takes quite a bit of getting used to. When it gets cold people living in the desert need long warm robes. When the wind blows and the flying sand stings, they are thankful for the long sort of scarf they have to wrap around their faces. However, the little camel in the picture is perfectly adapted for life in the desert. He's got those big padded feet which make it easier for him to walk on the soft sand. He's got long eye lashes to protect his eyes from flying sand. He's got a very smart trick of being able to close his nostrils when the sand whips about. He will soon begin to develop a bit of a hump and when he's fully grown he will have quite a big hump of fat. The hump is not water, it is fat. The fat releases water into the camel's system and so the camel is able to go for several days without drinking. Just how long without drinking depends on whether it's very hot or just warm or whether the camel has to work very hard or just amble around. But there is no doubt that the camel has made himself as comfortable as possible in rather harsh surroundings.

The camel is very useful to people living in the desert and they in turn help the animals. Humans will find food and water for the camel and the camel will carry the human's tent, his cooking pots and the things he has to sell. They would find it difficult to live without each other.

OSTRICH (above) Hurray we're out, now what are we going to do? I don't think it's much of a day for flying do you? No, it's not much of a day for flying and never will be much of a day for flying, because ostriches cannot fly. Ostriches are the biggest of all the birds and ostrich eggs are quite enormous. The shell is as thick as china. If you wanted to boil an ostrich egg you would have to give it a good hour.

These little ostriches are already the size of fully grown chickens and when they are adult, they might well be two to two and a half metres (seven or eight feet) tall and weigh 100 to 180 kilogrammes (two to three hundred pounds). These eggs were laid in a scratched out hole in the ground and both the hen and cock ostrich helped to incubate or hatch them. The cock ostrich, or father, will look after them. They live in the grasslands of Africa and some are found in the Sahara desert. There was a time when ostrich feathers were very fashionable—ladies liked to wear them in their hats and it was found that the best way to get these feathers was to keep ostriches in captivity. So ostriches were farmed and there was a tremendous trade in ostrich feathers. But, as happens with trends, the feathers went out of fashion. Ostriches are incredible runners and when they get into top gear they can knock up 50 kilometres (30 miles) an hour and keep going for a quarter of an hour without much trouble. So if you can run like that why bother to fly?

SEAS, SNOW
and
ICE

The oceans of the world cover about seven tenths
of its total area and millions of animals
have adapted themselves to living either in
the sea or on land close to the sea.
The Antarctic to us seems a terrible place to
choose to live. It is bitterly cold and the winds
can be dreadful and yet millions of penguins
and seals thrive there. The Arctic too is a
brutal place to settle down in but seals live there
and so do polar bears and grizzly bears.
In what seems to us a scene of awful desolation
they can all find something to eat.

SOUTHERN SEA LION (previous page) This little one is just resting on the black volcanic rock of the Galapagos Islands. He was probably born there and he could be asking his mother just what is the difference between seals and sea lions. They do look very much alike but there are certain differences that you can spot straight away. On dry land a sea lion can roll its back flippers underneath its body and then push on the flippers so that they roll out and drive him forwards. A seal cannot. It can only paddle itself along on land using its big front flippers and dragging its back flippers behind. The other difference that you will notice is that sea lions have ears which you can see. Seals have not.

The sea lion that you see doing tricks in a circus is generally the Californian sea lion and it is smaller than the Southern sea lion. Although this mother and baby seem to be on their own, the rest of the pack cannot be very far

away. They are controlled by one very large male who tells everybody that he is boss and if you don't believe him, he'll fight you for it. As you can see it's very hot on the Galapagos Islands. They are right on the Equator and so it won't be very long before these two will just go for a swim to cool off. Not only will the sea be very cool and comfortable it will also be full of fish to eat.

GRIZZLY BEAR (above) This one is starting off life with a horrible name in a way, for he is known as Ursus horribilis. Imagine your teacher saying to you 'Ursus horribilis, come out here at once!' Not very nice, is it? His other name is not much better — it is grizzly. He's having a bit of a job to plod through the snow and he seems to be all on his own, so perhaps he is grizzling. But he didn't get his name because he's grizzling or moaning or whining. No, grizzle in this case

BLACK-BROWED ALBATROSS (below) This young bird seems to have got a bit excited and lost his head. There's just him on his own with his mum. She lays a single egg and only once a year. If the egg is broken or comes to grief, well that's that. She doesn't lay another one. It will be some little time before he's able to take off and roam over the ocean. There are thirteen species of albatrosses and they all live in the southern hemisphere.

The albatross is a gliding bird and, in what appears to be a most mysterious way, it is able to float in the air without flapping its wings. It seems to be hanging on an invisible thread and can glide and glide for days and days. It uses the air currents to keep up aloft and is a most fascinating bird to watch. Some albatrosses have tremendous wing spans, as much as three metres (ten feet). The sooty albatross, between breeding seasons, flies and glides right around the world and that is something like 32,000 kilometres (20,000 miles). So if you want to tell this young albatross' fortune you could safely say, 'Young man, you are going to have a long life and soon you will be going on a long, long journey'.

means 'of a greyish colour' or 'mixed with grey'. So here we have a little mixed-with-grey bear that's mostly brown anyway.

There are countless stories about grizzlies: of how they would attack men on horseback and even kill bison. They were once fairly common in North America but not very many are left now and those are in Alaska. There's no doubt that the grizzly is a big bear and there is one interesting theory put forward about the size of bears. It is this — the closer you get to the Equator, the smaller the bears will be. Well the grizzly is one of the biggest of the bears. He lives in the far north and compared to the Himalayan and the Malayan bears, which live much nearer the Equator, he is much bigger. I expect that this little bear will soon find his mother, she can't be very far away. She will probably say to him 'Where have you been, you horribilis little bear?'

POLAR BEAR (above) This mother is quite a big mum since she may weigh over 300 kilogrammes (six or seven hundred pounds). Yet she produces a very tiny baby indeed, weighing about one kilogramme (between one and two pounds). You were much heavier when you were born: about four times heavier than a baby polar bear. At one time it was thought that a baby polar bear was quite able to survive the cold weather of the Arctic but in fact a baby polar bear will die if it is allowed to get cold. To prevent this, the mother polar bear makes a den in the snow just big enough for her to curl into and the warmth of her body makes that den very snug and warm. In this cosy den the baby is born and there he stays until he is big enough to come out into the cold Arctic snows. It used to be a very rare event for a baby polar bear to be born and survive in a zoo simply because the poor little thing was just not warm enough. People thought that polar bears liked it cold. But baby polar bears like it warm. Now that this is known, several polar bears are born and survive in zoos.

Polar bears eat seals. They can't catch seals in the water, they catch them on land. They are well camouflaged against the snow, that is they blend in with their surroundings. The only bit of a polar bear you can see is his big black nose. But he keeps his head down low, to keep it out of sight, and some say he even puts his big white paw over it when spying out the land.

TURTLE (right) Here's a comic little troop of green turtles. Some seem to be going one way and some the other. Normally they would all be going the same way, they would be heading out to sea. Their mother lays her eggs on a sandy sea shore, burying them deep in the sand and she probably lays more than a hundred of them. When the little turtles hatch out they make for the sea as quickly as they can, because there are all sorts of nasty creatures waiting to eat them before they get to the sea. So perhaps these little turtles were raised by man in safe surroundings.

The green turtle is its own worst enemy, although he couldn't possibly know it. The bald truth is that we love to eat it. It is a delicacy. And if you happen to be a delicacy in this hungry world, then your chances of surviving are not very good. There are many different sorts of turtle. Some of them grow to be very big indeed and the leatherback turtle seems to be about the biggest. Some have been captured weighing about a half a ton. Turtles can move through the water at surprising speeds and both the leatherback turtle and the green turtle have been timed at speeds of over thirty kilometres an hour (twenty miles an hour). If only the green turtle was as bad-tempered as the loggerhead turtle, he could frighten off those people who try to catch him. The loggerhead turtle can be a very awkward customer indeed and should you try to catch one, then you could be in the soup for a change.

KING PENGUIN These are really surprising birds. They have chosen to live in the most miserable part of the world. The young in this picture are the ones in the middle wearing the expensive-looking fur coats. But by our standards they lead anything but a life of luxury. To start with king penguins do not even build a nest. It is almost as though they want to make life even more difficult for themselves. Just one egg is laid. As you know, to incubate an egg, that is to help it hatch out, the egg must be kept warm. Well it's never, ever very warm in the Antarctic and sometimes it's stone-cold freezing. So the king penguin puts the egg on top of its feet and drops the lower part of its tum on top of the egg. And believe it or not that is how the king chick is hatched out. Both male and female take it in turns to incubate the egg. This allows them time to go off fishing. Once the chicks are left on their own they huddle together for warmth. The parents feed them till spring. Then the chicks lose their furs and grow their adult coats.

The king is a handsome-looking penguin and seems very proud of that spectacular orange colour at the side of the head. Penguins, of course, cannot fly in the air but they can fly along when they get in the sea. They use a strong, flapping motion and they can torpedo about as fast as a seal. The king penguin has got a rather posh relative who looks very much like him except that he's known as 'the emperor'. Kings and emperors and not a palace in sight.

WALRUS I wonder if they have had any oysters for their picnic on the shiny beach. This is a beautiful picture of two little walruses staying close to the big ones just in case. If you remember in Lewis Carroll's poem 'The Walrus and the Carpenter', the walrus says 'Oh, oysters come and walk with us'. Crafty old walrus! I don't think they get many oysters. However, they do eat all sorts of crabs and shell fish. They use those lovely ivory tusks to rake up their food from the ocean bed. The tusks are simply teeth that have grown down outside the mouth. The extraordinary thing is that they go on growing and growing. In fact the record walrus tusk is over one metre (three feet) long! It must be a bit worrying if you know that two of your teeth are going to keep on growing. Apart from using them for fishing, a walrus finds his tusks very useful for climbing steep chunks of iceberg and they are the most deadly weapons when the walrus is attacked. They are very big animals and weigh over a ton. So just imagine a ton of very angry walrus lunging at you with two terrible tusks and then tossing you lightly over his head. Well, a walrus has been known to kill a polar bear.

The female walruses have tusks as well as the males and they live a reasonably agreeable life up in the Arctic. They don't think much of us, because we have hunted them in the past. Now if you should see one, it is best not to go too close.

RIVERS
and
LAKES

Most rivers start off as quick-flowing little trickles
and gradually get bigger and slower.
Lots of animals use rivers for drinking water only and
some, like elephants, use rivers and lakes for
drinking and for wallowing and bathing.
The hippopotamus needs quite a big river to live in,
because he spends most of the day-time in the river
and only comes out to graze at night. Animals have
learned to use rivers for different purposes. For
instance, alligators hide on the banks of rivers waiting
to catch the ones that come to drink and beavers build
dams across rivers on which to build their lodges.

HIPPOPOTAMUS (previous page) The babies are born in the water. They kick out with their legs straightaway until they can find a place in the river or lake shallow enough for them to stand, so that their noses just stick out of the water. Hippos are really very efficient submarines. They have well-designed periscope eyes and snorkel noses. They can breathe and see when their two ton hulk is completely submerged. Sometimes it is very difficult to see them in the water because they can close up their snorkel noses, sink in the river and stay on the bottom for as long as ten minutes. Hippos like to be together and it is usual to see about fifteen or twenty of them soaking themselves.

Baby hippos are suckled in the water where they are fairly safe. Big hippos are very dangerous characters when threatened. So if you happen to be in a boat, it is best to steer clear of them. You can never be sure of what they are going to do: they are unpredictable. It is no trouble at all for them to tip your boat over and then champ about with their great jaws. Next time you visit a zoo just wait a minute or two for the hippo to open his big, cave-like mouth and you will see that he has enormous teeth. Wonderful defensive weapons. That is what they are used for, because the hippo doesn't have to kill for food. He eats grass. He is a grazer and he does his grazing at night. When the sun goes down, the hippos come out to graze and when the sun comes up they go back to the river for a day-long bath.

AMERICAN ALLIGATOR (left) You have got to admit that this young one looks quite attractive resting daintily on that big leaf. Alligators and crocodiles are very much alike and they spend their days in much the same way. The mother alligator lays perhaps twenty to thirty eggs on some rotting vegetation. She doesn't incubate the eggs herself but the warmth of the rotten vegetation helps to do this. The mother will guard her nest of eggs until they are hatched but after that the baby alligator is on his or her own. Like crocodiles, alligators are beautifully designed for the life they lead in the water. They are very clever at lying quite still with just their nostrils and eyes out of the water. Just waiting and watching for a nice lunch to come down to the water for a drink. If they feel like it they can submerge and close their nostrils and ears while they are under the water.

Alligators and crocodiles are tremendously strong and they are extremely dangerous at both ends. They have terrible jaws and one swish of their horny tail would fell quite a large animal to the ground. The American alligator has been hunted ruthlessly for its skin and was in danger of becoming extinct. However the shooting had to stop, and there are still some alligators left in America. I was once motoring in Florida and stopped at a petrol station. I got out of the car and there was an enormous alligator just sitting in the forecourt. The attendant said, 'He's alright. He comes up from the river most days.' However, I got back into the car, while it was being filled!

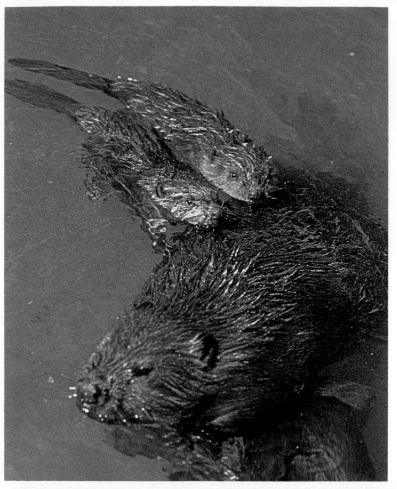

BEAVER (left) Now that's a nice, easy way of getting about. Two kits hang on to mum's fur, while she paddles about. These are little North American beavers and before long they will be taking lessons in building. Beavers are very clever construction engineers. They get their food and their building material more or less at the same time. They gnaw away at a tree until it falls to the ground. Now the beavers can get at the branches. They need the branches first of all to eat the bark, which forms part of their food and secondly to build their dam. The rest of their food comes from young tree shoots.

In the middle of the dam they build their lodge and that's where they will spend the winter. Beavers build dams to make artificial lakes with deep water. The entrance to the beavers' lodge is underwater with a sloping passageway leading up to it. They work very hard. They have no drawings, no tools and no ready-mix concrete delivered to the site, they just get on with it and the young ones learn from the older ones. Building a dam is far from easy. Beavers cannot drive stakes, so the branches are held down by stones and built up with more branches and stones and padded with mud. Beavers have been known to build a dam 450 metres (500 yards) long in a fast-flowing river. They are indeed most remarkable animals and in a few years time these two little beavers will be hard at it with their do-it-yourself kits.

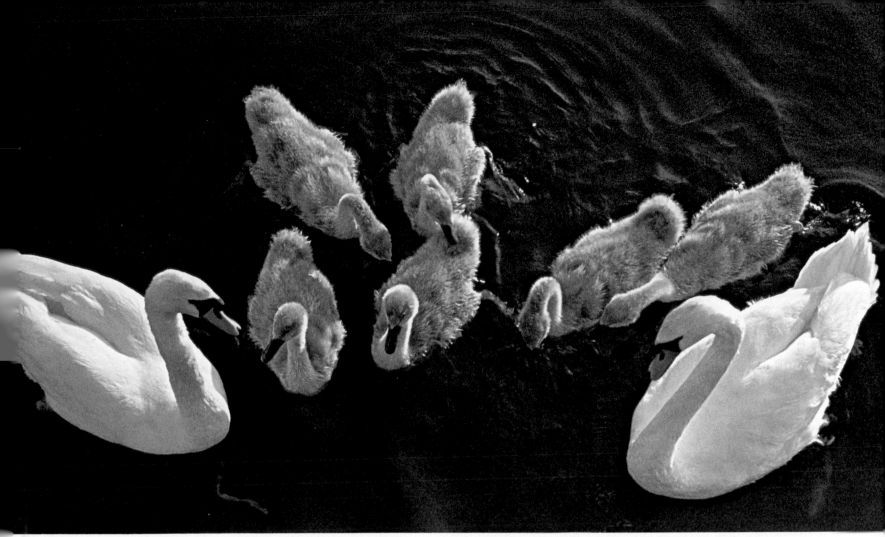

TOAD (left) Here are some amphibians. Don't be frightened by that word: it simply means a creature which has a varying body temperature, breathes air and can live both in water and on land. Many animals protect their young when they are born, they feed them and look after them, sometimes for several years, until they are quite grown up. But toads and frogs, the amphibians, and many reptiles just do not bother to do this. Instead of producing say one to six babies at a time they produce several thousands. They just lay the eggs and leave them to get on with it. The reasoning is that many will die but mercifully a few will survive.

In the picture you can see toads spawning. One female will lay as many as seven thousand eggs in long strings. You can see the strings of eggs strung up on bits of twig and weed. When the little ones hatch out they are absolutely on their own: no one to look after them. They don't need anyone to look after them. They become tadpoles and later turn into toads. And very strange lives they lead by our standards. Perhaps it's because they have never known their mums and dads but they do seem to like to sit alone under a stone and think things out. Perhaps they are wondering why they have so many warts. There are lots of fairy stories about toads. And no wonder. One toad was known to have sat underneath a doorstep for thirty-six years until it was accidentally killed. Of course it would have come from underneath the doorstep at night to feed in the garden on insects and slugs. Another toad was found down a coalmine. So there is just a touch of mystery about them.

MUTE SWAN (above) There is no need for me to tell you what an impressive picture it is to see a pair of swans and their family glide slowly down a river or across a flat, dark lake. The beautiful white swans and their 'ugly ducklings' that will eventually become as handsome as their parents. Swans lead very stable family lives. The parents stay together for life, a steady married couple. They both help to build the nest, although the female, known as the pen, does most of the building. The male, the cob, keeps up a watchful patrol while the pen is sitting on the eggs and he brings her food. Once the little cygnets are hatched, he will feed them and protect them. Swans can be dangerous when they are looking after their young. They have powerful necks and wings and have been known to attack humans in order to protect their cygnets. Although they are called mute swans, they will hiss dreadfully when angry. If anything frightens the cygnets while they are afloat they will hide in the wings on the back of father or mother. The family stays together throughout the year and then the young make off on their own, or if they feel a bit doubtful about going into the wicked world, they are driven firmly away by their parents.

You will find swans in many places where there is water. And where there is water people like to fish. But if you are keen on fishing don't leave any of that nylon line about, will you? Swans' necks and nylon fishing lines seem fated to get entwined with each other. The nylon line doesn't feel a thing. The swan suffers horribly.

CANADA GOOSE If you are a duck or a goose or a swan, you've got to be able to swim at a very early age, otherwise you will be in trouble. Once you are afloat you are fairly safe, as there aren't so many creatures about that would very much like to eat you, except perhaps a pike lurking about under the surface. These four little Canada geese are not much like their Mum and Dad, are they? However, they will lose that fluffy yellow down and take on the handsome black and white pattern that makes the Canada goose so very easy to spot. In Canada, where they come from, I have seen tremendous flocks of Canada geese. It is thought that they were introduced into this country about 200 years ago

and now they are fairly common here. Geese don't spend as much time in the water as swans but they do like to be close to water. They feed on grass and any bits of vegetation that take their fancy.

If geese don't like the look of you, they can put on quite a frightening 'I'm coming to get you' display. With necks stuck out and hissing like a steam engine, they have made many a brave man turn and run. The old farmyard goose was very good at doing this. It was also a wonderful watchdog, it would cackle away the moment a stranger appeared. These little Canada geese won't have to do that, for they've just got themselves to look after.

WOODS
and
FORESTS

Woods and forests are the homes of many creatures
because trees are very convenient things to climb up
when things get a little too dangerous on the ground.
Trees are also good places in which to hide
and of course they do provide a good shade.
Many of the creatures of the woods and forests are
very well camouflaged, so that they are difficult to
see in the flickering sunlight. The ones that go
hunting in the forest are lone hunters. The tiger
and the leopard are very good at stalking
the wild pig and deer that live in the forest.
Some forests can be quite dangerous for you and me.

AFRICAN ELEPHANT (previous page) If you are ever lucky enough to visit certain parts of Africa, you will very probably see a mother and baby elephant like this. They will be travelling in a herd with other females and their young: some a few months old and some a few years old. As you know, the elephant is the largest land mammal weighing up to six tons and the baby elephant, when it is born, weighs about 90 kilogrammes (200 pounds). It is quite a big baby. For about six months it lives on its mother's milk and gradually begins to eat grass, leaves and a twig or two. Father elephant has little to do with his family and generally prefers to look for food on his own or with one or two male friends. Now, supposing that you had taken this picture, what would you say would be the most sensible thing to do next? Well, if you were in a motor car, the most sensible thing would be to turn around quickly and drive away. If you were on foot — run for your life. There is no mistaking the big signal an African elephant gives when she is not at all pleased to see you. She signals with her ears. She sticks her big ears out and says, 'Now look here, if you don't buzz off pretty quickly, I'll be after you and you know what that means, don't you?' It simply means that she would kill you, that's all. Many people think that elephants are slow, gentle creatures. They may appear to be so in a zoo or a circus but in the wild they are extremely dangerous and they don't like us one little bit. It has been estimated by some people that they can move, when in a temper, at a speed of around 25 kilometres (15 miles) an hour. So have another quick look at those ears and put on your running shoes.

LEOPARD (right) If it were possible to present medals to wild animals for being the best runners, jumpers and climbers, then the leopard would qualify for one or two medals. It is a very good runner, a brilliant climber and an excellent jumper. Leopards are sometimes referred to as panthers and sometimes we hear people talking of black panthers. This is simply a leopard with a lot of black pigment in its coat. If you look closely at a black leopard or panther, you can still see the leopard spots beneath the black hair. Leopards are found in many places all over Africa, in India, China and Siberia. Black panthers mostly live in jungles in south-east Asia. The little leopard in the picture is probably having a lesson in hunting from his mother. Leopards have their own special way of hunting. To start with a leopard hunts alone and, like your cat at home, may do a very crafty belly crawl to get close to its prey and then wallop! Or it may just hide up in a tree and drop down on whatever passes by and takes its fancy. Then it often carries its kill up into a tree to have all on its own, out of reach of the hyenas and jackals. It sometimes happens that leopards, like lions and tigers, become man-eaters. They do become rather saucy, even going into houses and whipping someone out of bed and they simply love dogs. Not surprisingly, leopards are very unpopular with some people.

SPARROW HAWK (inset) It is now quite a common sight on long motor car journeys to see kestrel hawks hovering beside the motorway, although it does depend in which part of the country you are. The four chicks in the picture are not kestrel hawks but sparrow hawks. You will not see as many sparrow hawks as kestrels, for they do not hover and are therefore not so easy to spot. Like all birds of prey, sparrow hawks are great hunters. These four have a lot to learn and will have to grow a bit bigger before they are ready to fly off and catch their own food. They will have to be skilled at fast flying and swooping to catch other birds and small mammals to eat. Some people say that hawks are such cruel looking birds. Well, their talons are sharp and very strong, their beaks are certainly designed to rip things apart and they have incredible eyes. Eyes that can spot small birds and little mice from a long way away. How far away? Well, it has been calculated that a hawk's eyes are about eight times stronger than ours. So that's what gives the sparrow hawk its fierce look — not cruel — fierce, very fierce.

WILD BOAR (left) How many little ones can you count in the picture? Did you say nine? Well, there may be one or two more out of sight but that is an average number for a wild boar. Like the little baby tapir (see page 45), they have white stripes on their sides but as they grow older the stripes will fade away. These little pigs live in Germany. Two of them are taking a drink of milk. The others are doing what mum is doing: grubbing about for whatever is going for free. They will eat practically anything. They might even grub up a mole and that will be the end of him. They are excellent diggers. You may have seen domestic pigs in a field which has large bare patches. It has been dug up by the pigs. There is so much in the soil that they find simply delicious, they have to dig it up. The domestic pig was developed by us from the wild pig, because it was good to eat and because it was so simple to keep.

It's difficult to say just what will happen to these little wild pigs. They will be grown up in two years time and then they could be hunted for sport, or because they have damaged crops. The trouble with wild animals is that they just do not understand farmers. They cannot possibly know that those lovely potatoes growing in that field belong to farmer Smith. After all everything in the forest belongs to the wild pigs, they just don't know the difference.

PARADISE FLYCATCHER (left) There's just about enough room in this tiny nest for these two small birds. It's hard to believe that one day they will both look like the parent there. Both the birds are howling for food, as little birds always seem to be. The poor parent bird is just having a bit of a breather before flying off to find a few more flies. Flycatchers, as might be expected, are very clever at catching flies as they fly about. As you can see, when they are fully grown they have beautiful tails, which are often twice as long as their bodies.

You will never see a paradise flycatcher in this country but you may see a spotted flycatcher or a pied flycatcher. The spotted flycatcher is not such a wonderful show-off as the paradise flycatcher. In fact, it is rather an ordinary looking little brown bird and you would probably not notice it at all were it not for its funny fluttering flight. It perches fairly close to the ground and waits for a fly to fly by. Then it flies after it, grabs it and flutters back to its perch again. You probably didn't know that flycatchers are very fond of croquet. They don't play croquet, of course, but I have noticed that for many years now a spotted flycatcher has lived in my garden and it loves to perch on the croquet hoops in the lawn. The hoops are just right for the flycatcher. It flits from one to the other picking up flies as it goes. It is inclined to sulk a bit when we have a game of croquet because it cannot perch on its hoops.

KOALA (opposite) This baby could be your favourite teddy bear. It has a most engaging face and looks very cuddly. There was a time, not so very long ago, when the koala was on the verge of extinction, because millions of them were shot for their fur. Fortunately people realised what was happening and that the shooting had to stop, so the koala was made a protected animal.

There is normally only one baby born. He becomes as furry as his mother by the time he's six months old but he stays close to her for another six months. The one in the picture is clinging on tight to his mother who is half-way up a eucalyptus tree. He rides about on her back while she gathers her food. Koalas live in Australia where lots of eucalyptus trees grow and the strange thing about the koala is that it lives entirely on eucalyptus shoots and leaves. You would think it might like to try something else now and again. After all, I don't suppose you would be very happy living on, say, lettuce leaves all day long. However, the koala just sticks to eucalyptus leaves and hardly ever moves out of the eucalyptus trees. He sleeps at the top during the day and then wakes up to go and find the new and tender shoots to eat. In fact, they do say that the koala smells rather strongly of eucalyptus, which isn't surprising. The young koala will ride about on his mother's back until he's about a year old and then perhaps he will say goodbye and start a life all on his own in another beautiful, strong-scented eucalyptus tree.

TAPIR (inset) This little one will know very little about the wild sort of life he might have been living in Brazil or Malaysia. He is certainly much safer here, in a zoo. Tapirs are chunky, solid animals and they are a bit pig-like but they are not related to the pig at all. It is quite incredible that some tapirs live in South America, while thousands of kilometres across the sea, you can find others in Malaysia. They are slightly different from each other but not very much. The baby tapir is born with little white flecks all over but as it gets older these flecks will disappear. The peculiar thing about the tapir is its nose. It looks a bit like a sawn-off elephant's trunk and indeed it can swing it about quite a bit and this is helpful when it's out browsing. Tapirs generally come out at night to feed on leaves, fruit and grasses and spend most of the day lying up in the shade. They have got to be quite careful because there is one animal that is very fond of tapir for breakfast, lunch or supper and that is the jaguar. But it doesn't always get its own way. A tapir with a jaguar on its back will charge about through the bushes trying to smash the jaguar off its back. If that doesn't work, then the tapir might take a great dive into water and sink to the bottom. It can stay underwater longer than a jaguar.

ANTEATER (left) Do you ever wish you were an anteater? I don't suppose you do, because it cannot be a lot of fun just eating ants for breakfast, ants for dinner and ants for tea and supper. Much like eating crisps all the time but perhaps some people wouldn't mind that! The baby anteater in the picture is getting to be as big as his mother and yet she still carries him about on her back while she goes ant gathering. It must be an awfully fiddly business picking up ants but the anteater has developed a most efficient way of doing this. On its front paws it has some really dreadful claws. These are for ripping open ant hills and then the anteater puts its long, long sticky tongue into the ant hill and the ants just stick to the tongue like flies to a flypaper. I hope the little anteater is watching very carefully just how his mother catches ants, because he'll spend the rest of his life doing just that. There are some anteaters much bigger than the one in the photograph but this one lives in the trees and it has a tail that it can wrap around the branches to help it climb around. Now have you changed your mind about being an anteater? Well, when you get toothache you might wish you were one. Why? Anteaters do not have any teeth. Aren't they lucky?

RHESUS MONKEY (below) 'Right now, open wide and say Ahhhhh.' The big rhesus monkey is looking in the other one's mouth. I don't think that he's going to put a filling in one of her teeth. He probably wants to know what she has been eating lately. The big one is probably the boss of the group and what he says, goes. The little one there will have to do as he's told and if he doesn't, he gets punished. These monkeys are found in the forests and mountainous regions of India and South-east Asia and they move about in groups. The group is led by adult males, with females and young in the middle and young males at the back. They spend a certain amount of time grooming each other. It was thought that they were looking for fleas but it is now known that this is not altogether so. They are picking out bits of dead skin, perhaps a flea or a few lice. Monkeys like to be together, roaming about together, sitting close together and grooming one another. All is peace and quiet at grooming time. It's rather like being at the hairdressers. You sit quietly while the hairdresser carefully combs your hair. And then it's your turn to groom the hairdresser. Then the hairdresser turns to cousin Charlie and Auntie Gwen picks carefully through Uncle Bert's tangled mop. This way you get to know each other very well indeed. Rhesus monkeys are often kept as pets but like all monkeys they have quick tempers and very, very nasty bites.

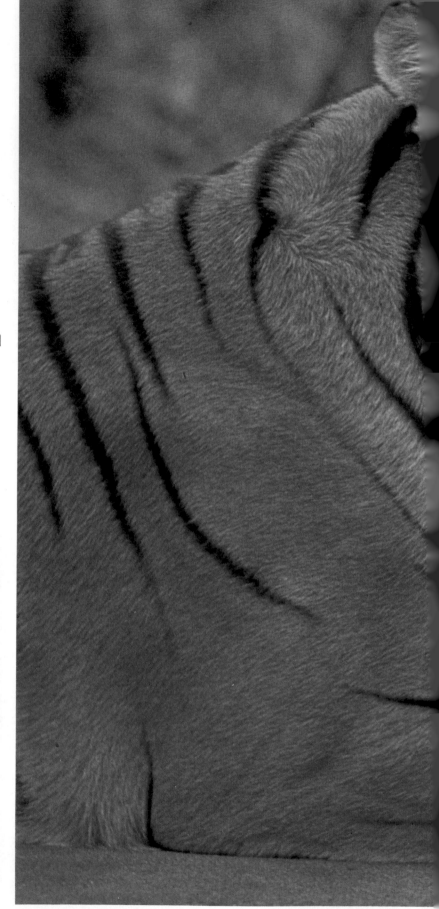

TIGER (right) They do say that if you were to lay the skeleton of a lion beside the skeleton of a tiger it would be very hard to tell the difference. But even though they are so similar in bone structure, the lion and the tiger are very different in many other respects. Lions live together in prides. They are what is known as social animals. Tigers are solitary animals. They like to be alone. They usually hunt alone. They spend a lot of time on their own. They are not all that keen on stopping and chatting with other tigers. The male and female do meet from time to time of course and the outcome can be as many as six little tigers. They are born in the spring of the year and usually in a place which is difficult for other creatures to find, since they are blind and helpless to start with and mother has to leave them now and again to go hunting. They look just like their father and mother and right from when they are born they have those

lovely stripes, that look as though they have been painted on with a smooth, black brush. When they are a few weeks old and have got over their wobbles, they start to play. Mum is very patient and flicks her tail about so that they can creep up and pounce on it. It's all very good practice for when they will have to hunt for themselves.

Tigers are forest dwellers but strangely enough cannot climb trees. Lions can. Tigers use the shady cover of the trees to creep up on a wild pig or a deer. Unfortunately quite a lot of forests are now being cut down for firewood or to make room for farming. So you see there are not nearly so many little tigers about as there used to be. If you cut down the trees in which the wild pig and the deer like to hide, then there is nowhere for them to live. If there are no wild pig and deer, there is nothing for the tiger to eat. And so the tiger is in danger of becoming extinct.

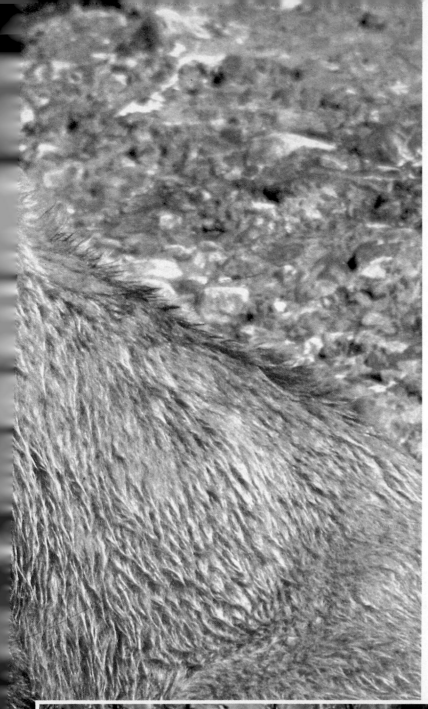

BEAR (left) There are still bears living in Europe and in the Soviet Union but I doubt very much if you would ever see one if you went looking for them. Bears are generally shy creatures and keep out of the way of things that smell like a man. Of course they can become very bold at times. In some parts of America the bears that live in the forests are tempted to come down to the main roads and plunder the litter bins for the scraps left there by motorists. And it is when bears become used to human beings that they get dangerous. Bears may look like friendly, cuddly creatures but they are quite the opposite. They have very quick tempers, as some people have found out to their cost.

These young bears will spend a very casual sort of life roaming about, eating pretty well anything. They are what is called ominivorous. So although they usually eat berries, fruit, bits of grass and a few leaves, they might try a salmon. Then, having eaten very well indeed all through the summer, bears do a very sensible thing, they curl up in a den and go to sleep. This is called hibernating. They may not sleep all through the winter. They will probably come out and have a prowl around if the sun is shining and then go back and nod off again for a week or two provided they are left alone. And most creatures very sensibly leave bears well alone.

RACCOON (inset) This one is just six weeks old. He looks as though he has his burglar's mask on and he's probably off to do some burgling. When he's grown up he will be about the size of a large cat but he will be able to do lots of things that cats cannot do. To start with he will be as nimble and quick in the trees as a squirrel. And he loves water. Raccoons never like to be too far away from water and they are strong swimmers. They are nocturnal animals, they lie up during the day and come out at night. Raccoons live in North America and are as bad as foxes for they will raid poultry houses. To some people they may seem a little fussy, because they like to wash their food before they eat it. They take it to the water's edge and roll it around in their front paws. Some food is ready-washed for they do like to eat crayfish. A zoo keeper I know sometimes gives one of his raccoons a lump of sugar. You should see the look on that raccoon's face when he takes the lump down to the water and starts to wash it. He simply cannot believe that it is disappearing right in front of his masked eyes.

MOUNTAINS and ISLANDS

Mountains and islands can be fairly safe places on which to live simply because they are often quite difficult to get at. Animals that live on mountains are very sure-footed. They can bound about the rocks and leap across the gullies. They can also make do with the small amount of food there is on mountains. Animals that live on certain islands very often have calm and peaceful lives, because there are no predators on the island. Predators are animals that catch and eat other animals. Where the predators are kept away and the rest are left in peace, they can grow very large like the giant tortoises of Galapagos and Aldabra.

GIANT TORTOISE (previous page) That's the idea, keep up the good work, you'll soon be out of your egg shell and ready to settle down to a nice long life. Curiously, many species found on islands are different from those found on big continents. The islands that lie about 1000 kilometres (600 miles) west of Ecuador, the Galapagos Islands, are well known for the fact that a great number of animals there are unlike those on the mainland. Indeed in some cases they are unlike anything found anywhere else. The marine iguana is such a one. The giant tortoise, however, is also to be seen on the island of Aldabra in the Indian Ocean.

It could take about forty years for the baby giant tortoise to become a big giant tortoise. He will have to eat up his greens if he wants to grow. Then he will get bigger and bigger and could eventually weigh as much as 200 to 250 kilogrammes (4 to 5 hundredweight). In the days of sailing ships, when it was difficult to get fresh meat, it was found that the giant tortoise was a most convenient animal to keep on board and have for Sunday lunch. It was easy to keep, it didn't need feeding and it was very good meat. So sailors plundered the islands for years and years and the tortoise population went down. Then dogs were introduced and the eggs and the young were eaten and the population went down a lot more. Fortunately the giant tortoise is now being reared successfully, so the little one just coming out of his shell may live for a hundred years more.

WILD GOAT (above) Now here's a very cosy couple. The kid will have been born in April or May and may have one or two twin brothers or sisters. They are happy to be high up in the unfriendly mountains as this wild goat and child are perfectly adapted to this sort of life. They've got it all worked out. You've only got to look at them to realise that they know perfectly well that they don't have to build a house, they don't have to go shopping, they don't have to do any cleaning or washing. They will get up when they feel like it and they will pick a bit of greenery when they feel like it. These goats live in the mountains of Asia Minor and they are far from being silly billy goats. Although they don't look it now, they are fast climbers. They know exactly how to keep out of harm's way for they are able to live at heights of over 3,000 metres (10,000 feet), so you would have to be very keen and clever if you wanted to catch one of these wild goats.

The domestic goat was probably bred from these wild goats and in some countries the domestic goat is a very valuable animal. It is used in the same way that we use a cow. In relation to its size, a domestic goat gives almost three times as much milk as a cow. The milk is easier to digest and of course it can be made into butter, yoghourt and cheese. There are many famous cheeses made from goats' milk. The two in the picture seem to say, 'Ah, but you've never tasted Wild Goats' Cheese, have you?'

ALPINE IBEX (above) These two could be twins and they are certainly out together for a bit of a frolick. They are quite lucky to be alive at all really, because, as has happened with so many animals, the ibex very nearly became extinct. Once again it's the old, old story of the gun being much more efficient than the bow and arrow. Why would anyone want to kill an ibex? Well, in three or four years time these two little ones will have grown into big and beautiful animals. They will have brown horns that could be as much as one metre (three feet) long. So ibexes were shot for their meat and they were shot because people like to put their magnificent horns on the walls of their homes. They are called trophies. Nothing to be proud of, to have your walls covered in trophies. However, the shooting of ibexes is forbidden and has been for some time. So now there are herds of them in the Italian, Swiss, French, Austrian and Yugoslavian alps.

Ibexes, like most goats, are very sure-footed and are very clever jumpers and leapers. These two were able to climb only a few hours after they were born. They have got a tough but pleasant life in front of them. They graze the mountain slopes and when the weather gets hot they'll move higher up the mountain where it is cool and when the temperature drops they'll wander down to a warmer spot.

BALD EAGLE (left) It's difficult to say whether these birds enjoy being called bald eagles. However, they certainly look bald because of their white heads and they certainly are called bald. The bald eagle chicks you can see in their nest will no doubt grow up to be very handsome and proud looking birds. Their nest is high up in a tree top in the United States of America and, although they probably don't know it, the bald eagle is the national bird of America. They feed mainly on fish.

Eagles are extremely powerful birds and there are many stories of them carrying off lambs, young deer and goats and even little children. So you had better wear your heaviest boots when you go to the mountains where the eagles live. However, I wouldn't worry too much, because most of the stories you hear about eagles carrying off children are not true. In fact, there is only one true case of an eagle making off with a little girl and that happened in Norway. Fortunately, the little girl was just a bit too heavy and the eagle had to drop her before it got to its nest. The girl escaped with a few scratches and bruises. There is one very true thing, though, about the bald eagle. It builds one of the biggest nests in the world. It adds to the nest year after year and one great nest in Ohio, which crashed in a storm, was over two and a half metres (eight feet) wide and four metres (twelve feet) deep and weighed something like two tons!

MOUNTAIN ZEBRA (above) Take a good look at this little one because he is a very rare one indeed. He is the smallest of all the zebras and we are very lucky to see this picture of him because the mountain zebra is almost extinct. It is quite alarming how quickly and easily certain species of animals become extinct. Two hundred years ago one of the most numerous of the zebra family was a species called the quagga. It was striped only over the head and neck and part of the body and it was a very beautiful animal. But it was hunted and shot until there were only a few quaggas left dotted about in zoos. There was a bit of a panic when people realised that the only quaggas in the world lived in zoos but it was too late to save them. And the last quagga in the world died in Amsterdam Zoo just about a hundred years ago. That was a very sad thing for the quaggas and for us. The same fate nearly overtook the mountain zebra but fortunately people realised in time that it was on the way out and it is now a protected animal. Even so there are probably less than one hundred of them left.

In the past, the Romans used to call the zebra the horse-tiger and the future for this little horse-tiger is probably quite good. He seems to be in very good condition and is quite happy to stand still while those two little birds, ox-peckers, hop around him pecking away at all the irritating creatures that hide in his long hair. He's enjoying it, isn't he?

FIELDS
and
BURROWS

Next time you go for a walk in the country
you will be lucky if you get so much as a glimpse
of a rabbit or a hare. Not so long ago there were
rabbits everywhere and in wintertime you would
see hares racing away over the downs. Both disease
and modern farming methods have reduced the
number of wild animals in the hedgerows and fields.
But several have survived and they are still a most
important part of countryside life. The grass eaters
fill up with grass. And where there are grass eaters
there will be eaters to eat the grass eaters.
It's a very old cycle of life.

POLECAT (previous page) These babies still have their eyes closed but it should not be long before they are open and in about five months time they will be fully grown. It is very difficult to say but there are probably no more polecats left in England or Scotland but there are some in Wales. The polecat has been domesticated and been bred into what we call a ferret.

Ferrets have been used for years to help us catch rabbits. A good ferret was worth quite a bit to the countryman because he relied on it to catch some of his food. The ferret was simply put into a rabbit warren and the frightened rabbits would bolt. They were either caught in nets as they dashed out of their holes or they were shot. There was a time when pretty well every cottage in the country had a little ferret hutch tucked away around at the back but there aren't very many about today. It often happened that when a ferret was put into a rabbit warren it wouldn't come out. Some warrens were very deep and no matter how hard you dug you couldn't find your ferret. The ferret had probably caught a rabbit, eaten it and gone to sleep. So it was given up as lost. But the ferret was quite able to look after itself feeding on rabbits, frogs and rats and eventually became wild. It probably bred with the wild polecat. These little polecats will become very fierce and they will develop that astonishing trick that the stoats and weasels also do so well. If attacked by a dog or a cat they do make a most awful pong. It's enough to put you off.

BROWN HARE (left) Perhaps it's almost time to run and hide. He has seen somebody moving about and he thinks that maybe he'd better get out of the way. Hares are very beautiful animals and if you ever see one you will be astonished at its powerful grace and terrific speed. A hare can manage 70 kilometres (45 miles) an hour when pushed and funnily enough it runs better when it's going uphill. This is because it has long back legs that move together and shorter front legs. A hare is not so happy running downhill as it hasn't such good control.

The little hare is called a leveret and he's quite able to look after himself when he's just about a month old. He likes to eat clover and cabbage leaves. Unlike rabbits, hares do not make burrows: they live on top of the ground. However, they are very good at hiding and they do this by scooping out a sort of dish in the ground and they lie in this dish with their ears back flat. They are very difficult to see. The place which they make to lie in is called a form and they make sure that their form is in a place where they can keep a good look out. A hare will not move from its form unless you get very close to it and then it's gone in a flash. It will have watched you coming in its direction for a long time and then decided, when you were a few yards away, that it was time to be off. The little leveret in the picture may one day be a 'Mad March Hare'. They are so called because in the early part of the year the jack hares (the males) congregate and fight over who's wife shall belong to whom.

HORSE (above) Once upon a time there were more horses in this country than there were human beings. The horse was a most important domestic animal, that is an animal which was kept to work for us. The little foal there with its mother wouldn't know anything about that, of course. We have tamed and used horses throughout the world for thousands of years. The Chinese almost certainly rode horses as long ago as 3000 B.C. So we have had plenty of time to develop the wild horse into all sorts of tame and domesticated horses. Now there is only one type of wild horse left and this is called Przewalski's horse. The mother and foal in the picture are roaming free on the plains of America. They are called mustangs and belong to a herd of horses. A long time ago they were once domesticated horses but they escaped and they are now wild again.

We used to breed horses for riding about, horses to pull light carts, horses to pull ploughs and harrows, horses to pull delivery vans and horses to go to war. In fact, there was hardly anything in this life that we could accomplish without horses. Then came the internal combustion engine with motor cars, buses and aeroplanes and we said to the horse, 'Thanks very much but that's your lot'. Fortunately, we didn't get rid of all our horses and we still have a few of all the breeds of which there used to be millions. It is important to be a good judge of horse flesh, so that you buy the right horse for the right job. Would you choose this little one?

FOX (left) What has he seen? He's just sizing up the situation and then perhaps he will do his famous little jump in the air and pounce on that whatever-it-is under the leaves. It may only be a beetle or an earwig but it's all good practice. He will need all the practice he can get, because before long quite a lot of people will be after him. He was probably born in an old rabbit burrow that his mother, the vixen, thought would do very well as a nursery. When the cubs were born the father, the dog fox, would often bring food to them. The little foxes grow quickly and by the time they are three months old they will be wandering off on their own, exploring this and that and finding out a lot about the countryside. At six months the little fox is just about as big as his mum and it won't be long before he leaves home. He'll find plenty to eat, such as voles, mice, slugs, snails, rabbits and rats. Some foxes have been known to steal chickens and it must not be forgotten they they'll eat windfall apples and perhaps a few blackberries.

Many people think that the fox does nothing but harm, others think he is a very worthy animal and needed to help maintain the balance of nature. There is certainly no doubting his intelligence and his cunning.

RABBIT (inset) Here is an irresistible little creature. He was born in a burrow that his mother had prepared with nice soft materials including some of the fur from her own body. He probably had three or four brothers and sisters born at the same time. Their mother looked after them very well indeed, going out to graze and coming back every now and again to feed them her milk. At one month old this one was big enough to look after himself and before very long his mother would be having more babies. Rabbits can have four litters in a year and that makes an awful lot. Hundreds of rabbits used to live together in one warren. They ate a lot of corn and you could see fields with great bare patches that the rabbits had cleared. There were so many rabbits in spite of all the enemies they had. Foxes, stoats, weasels: they were all after rabbits and were helped by men with traps and guns. But the rabbit won. Until a disease called myxomatosis came along and killed off most of the rabbit population. Now there are still rabbits about but they do not generally live in warrens as they used to.

FARMS
and
MEADOWS

It is a very fortunate thing that we still have
some of the very early breeds of domestic animals
in this country. Our ancestors, when they gradually
stopped roaming about and settled down probably
took wild pigs from the forest and tamed them.
They did not have to hunt them any more, for they had
them under control to do what they liked with them.
Then they began to 'improve' them: to breed different
types together, so that they grew bigger much faster.
But in some cases the tough sturdy qualities
were bred out. So it is a fortunate thing that we still
have some of those tough breeds about just in case.

JERSEY COW (previous page) The domestic cow is a most remarkable animal. Here is a beautiful Jersey calf. He's probably had a good feed and is now doing just what it ought to do — having a nice lie down. When a cow calves, she comes into milk and she produces enough milk for her calf. But we have changed things a bit. Through breeding we have produced cows that give enough for their calves but a lot for us as well. In fact we very nearly take the lot and sometimes you will hear a farmer say to his cowman, 'Don't leave too much for the calf, he's a greedy little so-and-so'. But I would imagine that the little calf in the picture will run free with his mother and be allowed to take as much milk as he wants.

In Jersey the cows are very often milked in the field. Of all the cows, they are the most delicate looking and have the most sensitive faces. They have kind faces and that's not as silly as it sounds, because some cows have most unkind faces and they are hardly ever good milkers. In Jersey, when the weather is a bit on the chilly side, the farmers put long coats on their cows, so that they do not feel the cold. Well, if you have a cow with a kind face, the least you can do is to be kind to the cow.

ARAUCANA CHICKEN (right) Just for fun, try to imagine that when you were a tiny little baby, you were stolen from your cot by a gang of chimpanzees and they took you off to live in a forest where there were no humans. If you survived then you would grow up thinking that you too were a chimpanzee, because you would not remember your early days with human parents. This is a bit unlikely to happen to you but it is often the case that young creatures are brought up by 'foster parents'. This means parents who take over from the real mother and father. It frequently happens in the poultry world. The foster mother in the picture is a bantam and the little chicks are araucana chicks. They are a breed of rather fancy looking birds that come from South America. As you know, when a hen bird goes 'broody' it means that she has laid all the eggs that she wants to lay and is now preparing to sit on them to hatch them out. But sometimes, for many different reasons, the broody hen's eggs are taken away and she is given eggs of a different species to sit on. When the eggs hatch out, the broody hen believes the chicks to be her very own and the chicks believe the broody hen to be their proper mother. She will look after them although within an hour after they are hatched, the chicks can stand, peck up their own food and even run about.

Farmyard chickens have hatched out ducks' eggs and looked after the little ducklings very well. But I know someone who made a big mistake when he put some chicken's eggs under a broody duck. The chicks hatched out and the mother duck took what she thought to be her ducklings for a swim. It was very sad. The little chicks followed her and were drowned. So you've got to be careful.

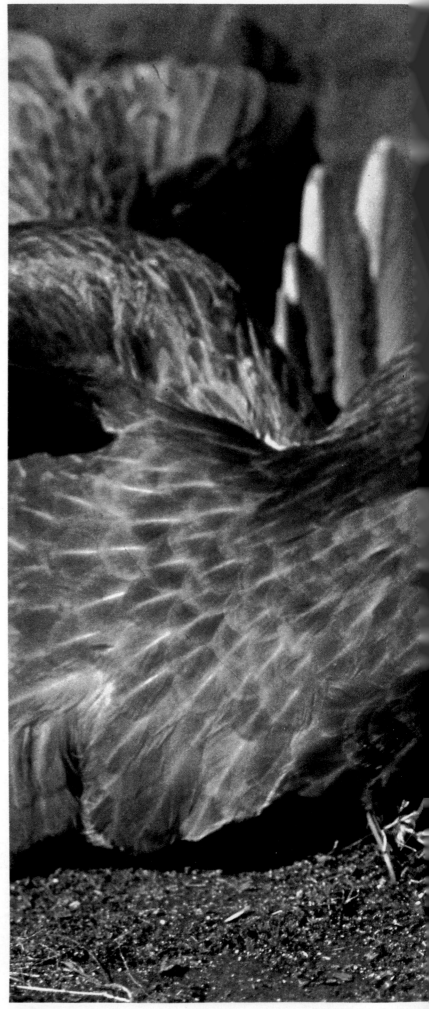

DOMESTIC DUCK (above) These are often described as being very funny birds. They are in many ways. They have funny voices that sometimes sound as if they are laughing very sarcastically. They also seem to get in a bit of a dither now and again. These funny qualities were taken up by the creators of Donald Duck when they put him in a sailor suit and hat. Ducks are rather awkward walkers, they waddle in a ponderous way but the moment they get on the water they lose their awkwardness and become very graceful swimmers.

The domestic duck was bred from the wild duck and one way and another we have produced some extraordinary looking breeds of duck. The adult here is an Aylesbury duck, with two ducklings of her own, the yellow ones, and two Mallard ducklings. The one thing they can all do, of course, is swim the moment they are hatched out. These little ducklings have a lovely lake to swim on but ducks can exist without water to swim on. When ducks are hatched in an incubator and have never seen their natural mother they can become very attached to one of the first things they see. I know some ducks that became very attached to a pair of striped socks worn by the young lady who fed them. They were very bright blue and white football socks and it didn't matter who wore the socks, the little ducks would follow those socks everywhere. They would make very loyal football supporters.

SHEEP (right) Any little lamb looks just like another little lamb except to its mother. Every mother sheep knows its own lamb, although not every lamb knows its own mother. Should he try to drink from a sheep that isn't his mother, she will soon tell him he's made a mistake and butt him on his way. We have used sheep for thousands of years and the domestic sheep here are certainly descended from wild sheep. We realised a long, long time ago that the wool on a sheep was a most wonderful material. It is most comfortably soft and warm and, until fairly recently, without sheep's wool, we would have shivered a bit.

In this country we have bred all sorts of sheep and we became very rich because of the wool we sold to other countries. The sort of sheep a farmer keeps depends on the sort of country the farmer lives in, for sheep can vary a great deal. There are sheep that live best in the mountains because they are tough and can survive on the sparse grass. There are sheep that live best on lower ground and grow long wool. In fact there are many breeds of sheep that are best for wool and many that are best for meat and there are some that are good at producing both wool and meat. Do you think that the sheep in the picture is sure that the little lamb is hers? It sometimes happens that a little lamb loses his mother, then it has to be brought up in the farmhouse and is given milk in a bottle, until it's old enough to look after itself.

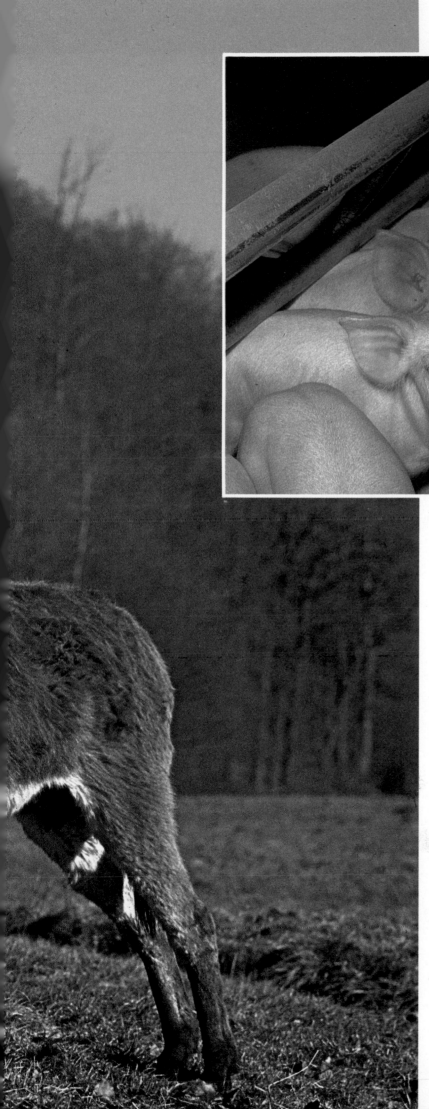

PIG (inset) To us this is one of the most useful of animals. It will eat pretty well anything and when it is dead we can eat pretty well every bit of it. The domestic pig is descended from the wild boar. From that wild boar we have experimented and bred all sorts of different pigs. Some were longer, some got fatter quicker, some were much more hardy, some were on the delicate side. The French bred different types and so we took some of the French pigs and bred them with some of ours. In other words what we are trying to get is the biggest, quickest-growing, strongest pig. But then it mustn't be too fat and it mustn't be too coarse. We are never satisfied. The little pigs in the picture couldn't care less what we expect of them. They are concerned with nothing much except feeding themselves. They will grow very quickly. From being about one kilogramme (just over a couple of pounds) at birth they will grow to getting on for 4 kilogrammes (nine pounds) in a fortnight.

DONKEY (left) If you happen to have a bit of a paddock next to your house, you can do a lot worse than invite a donkey to come and live in it. They are most interesting animals. This little foal will have a nice long coat by the time the winter comes but even with the coat he will need a shed to shelter in and so will his mother. Donkeys originally came from Africa and although they have lived in Europe for quite a time, they still have not learned to get absolutely used to the cold. They need a bit of shelter. Apart from that and a little bit of feed during the winter, they ask for nothing and provide a good deal of fun.

Donkeys know a lot of things but they aren't going to tell you. They will just stand there and think about what they might do next week if the weather is fine. And that could be anything. They like being talked to and will listen quietly even if you talk to them about algebra or Latin or arithmetic. The people of some countries rely on the donkey quite a lot for moving things around. They hang baskets on either side of the donkey and load him up with everything: fruit, maize, firewood and loads of stone for roadmaking. Sometimes you may see a small haystack moving down the road towards you. Somewhere at the bottom of that haystack is a donkey.

HOMES
and
GARDENS

For thousands of years now we have always found
it a great advantage to have animals close to us.
Without dogs we would not have been very
successful at hunting and when we started to
grow crops and store grain, we found that
cats were very useful indeed for catching
rats and mice. The dog is no longer a hunter because
there's not much left for him to hunt, but the
cat still finds quite a bit to do in most homes and
gardens. We have two other friends in
the garden, where they are in their own environment
— the hedgehog and the robin.

ROBIN (previous page) 'Come on, sing up my dears, you've got to practise your Christmas carols.' Quite a lot of young birds open wide and say 'Ah' when the parent bird comes to the nest. So the one that shouts the loudest and opens widest often gets the titbit. Even if you can't tell a rook from a crow or an ostrich from an emu, you must be able to recognise a robin. That is, an adult robin, because the juvenile robin does not have that red breast.

Robins are known to be very matey birds. They seem to be quite tame and sometimes when you are digging in the garden, a robin will hop around quite close to you, waiting to see if you are going to turn up something for him. He means to get it before anyone else. They are amusing little birds too in the way that they will choose old places to build their nests. They will perhaps pick on an old flower-pot lying on its side in the porch or an old shoe box in the garage and they might make a nest in an old boot if it is tucked away somewhere handy. They do seem to like something different and original. They like to make a nest in the things we have forgotten about. Their nests are roughly put together and are cup-shaped. A robin will nest in a hedgerow, of course, or in holes in walls and it will rear from four to seven little ones. There is just one more endearing little habit out of the robin's many charming ways. It sings all the year round. We do appreciate that.

GUINEA PIG (right) These little ones are just a day old and you must agree they are a lot prettier at this age than day-old mice (see page 74) and they can see the moment they are born. Guinea pigs were once kept by the Incas of Peru in South America a long, long time ago and, it is believed, they were brought to Europe shortly after South America was discovered. They obviously looked something like the ones in the picture but we have altered the guinea pig's appearance such a lot by breeding that you can now get guinea pigs of many different colours and with many different types of fur.

Guinea pigs are very good-natured little rodents and unlike most rodents (such as mice, gerbils and hamsters) do not produce masses of babies every year. They have two or three litters every year, with about four babies each. They live for four to five years. They need pretty much the same housing conditions as rabbits, see page 78, save that the cage need not be as big. It must have its private bedroom and it needs to be cleaned out every day, that is, the droppings and any stale food should be taken out. The whole cage should be cleaned out once a week and it is a good idea to disinfect once a month. They do need a bit of exercise and you could arrange the hutch so that it will open up into a wired run. Or, if you have time, it's best to let him have a run on his own on the grass but do make sure first of all that your dog or cat is used to him and won't chase him or worry him. Guineas like bran and oats, a little fruit, carrot, dandelion leaves and clover.

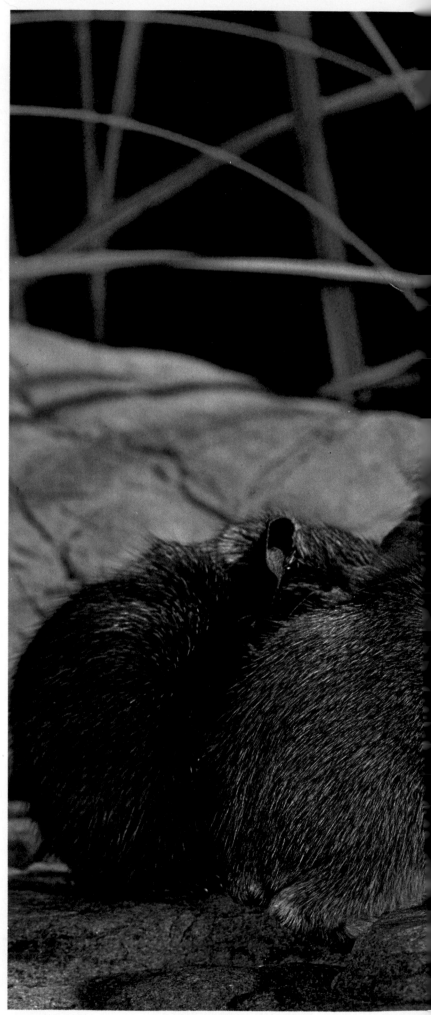

WHITE MOUSE There are many people who are afraid of mice, there are many people who cannot stand the sight of them and not so very long ago well brought-up ladies used to faint at the sight of a mouse. We put down mouse traps to catch mice simply because they do a lot of damage. They are naughty little nibblers. They will nibble at bags of flour, they will nibble at the packet of biscuits, they will nibble at the box of macaroni. They spoil far more than they eat. But if you can forget these nasty little goings-on and regard a mouse for what it is, you will perhaps appreciate that it is a very pretty and sensitive little animal.

White mice like the one in the picture are very attractive little creatures. As you can see her babies are very bald but in a few weeks they will look very much like their mother. They are not hard to keep but they must be given a decent house in which to live. A metal cage is the best sort of accommodation as mice are inclined to gnaw away at wooden cages. It is also important to have a little upstairs room that is nicely private. Animals like to hide themselves now and again and they feel safe in a closed bedroom. There will, of course, be a little sloping ramp up to their private room. Mice seem to be very fond of playthings which indeed do stop them from getting bored. They do love a revolving wheel to run around in. Be warned, however, if you have a male and a female white mouse, you could soon have more white mice than you know what to do with.

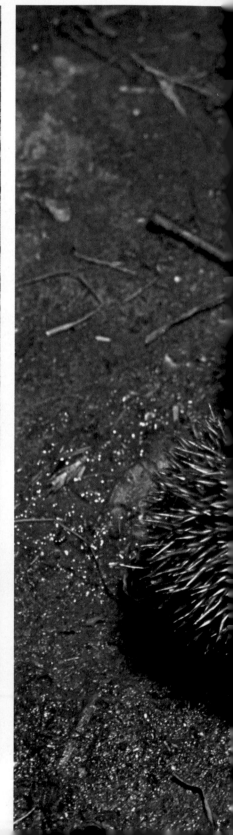

74

HEDGEHOG Here's a prickly little quartet and they know exactly what they like. Put down a saucer of water and a saucer of milk and the hedgehog will choose the milk. There are lots of people who put out a little food for hedgehogs and they do become quite regular in their habit of calling in the evening for a little refreshment. Unfortunately for hedgehogs they do not understand this modern world at all. They still think that they are living in the days of the horse and cart and do not realise how fast and dangerous is the modern motor car. Sadly nowadays you see more dead hedgehogs than live ones. However, you may still find one in your garden. You will probably hear him before you see him for hedgehogs feed at dusk and right through the night. They are rather noisy little animals. They go snuffling about and will eat all manner of things, including adders.

The hedgehog's favourite trick is to roll himself up into a ball. Well perhaps it's not his favourite trick because he does this when he is in danger and when he's rolled up he is very difficult to deal with. It takes a very clever dog to unroll a hedgehog. Game-keepers do not like hedgehogs because they say they eat pheasants' eggs but then game-keepers only like pheasants and distrust pretty well anything else that moves. It is said that a hedgehog has 16,000 prickles. I don't know whether this is true so next time you see a hedgehog you might like to count its spikes to check.

CAT (inset) One of the nicest things about this life is that we have the wonderful companionship of cats and dogs. This kitten is a beautiful little animal and no matter how it behaves, it is a joy just to look at. Of course all dogs and cats must be taught to behave. A quick tap and a sharp 'No' and they will soon get the message. You can buy some excellent claw sharpening posts and make a litter tray which kitty will soon learn to use. Also, it will be delighted to master the art of going in and out of the cat flap whenever it pleases. Kittens need feeding three or four times a day and when the meal is finished then the dishes should be taken up and cleaned. When the kitten is about six months old, then it need only be fed twice a day, in the morning and in the evening. Routine is a very good thing to follow with all animals. Don't be upset if your cat just ignores you and walks away from you when you call it. Cats are like that, they will choose their own time and place to be friendly and affectionate.

DOG (left) No doubt you would like to take this little one home with you. It is always a great temptation to want to care for little puppy dogs, because they look so appealing. The first thing that you must think of is whether you know what the puppy is going to grow into. If you know what his mother and father were like, then you can get a good idea of how the puppy will turn out. Only choose a dog that you know you can house and exercise properly. All dogs need exercise but some need much more than others. Big dogs need a lot. The other most important thing is that you must be prepared to train your dog. You can get advice on this. You will need a lot of patience because it is quite a long business and it is most important that your dog is properly trained. An untrained dog is an abomination.

There are some people I know and like very well indeed but they have badly behaved dogs. Dogs that jump up at you with filthy feet, dogs that have their noses into everything you put on the table, dogs that yelp all the time. I would rather not know these dogs and sadly their owners. So if you have friends that like you, make sure that they will like your dog too.

SPUR-THIGHED TORTOISE (above) They do say that if you have a tortoise and it gets out of your garden or its box you may be sure that it is heading south. So all you have to do is walk in a southerly direction loudly calling out its name. You may be lucky. But I do not think that these little tortoises will wander very far for a while. They will be quite happy to stay with the larger ones. They are called spur-thighed tortoises simply because they have a hard spur on their thighs. They come from around the Mediterranean and they are the smallest of all the tortoises.

In cold weather they get less and less active and will hibernate, that is, go to sleep for the winter. But be careful. If you have a tortoise and it is a small one do not make it hibernate. A little tortoise will not have enough flesh about it to last the hibernation. That is why so many tortoises are discovered in the spring to be still and lifeless. A good guide is to measure the underside of your tortoise. If it is under about seven centimetres (three inches) long, then keep it warm through the winter and feed it. The summer is no problem at all. Make it a little box with a wire run and give it a nice variety of green leaves and fruit, such as dandelion leaves, clover and grass clippings, grapes, cherries and tomatoes. If you have a garden from which a tortoise cannot escape then let him loose and see which way he goes. If he heads for the south just tell him he'll come to the English Channel if he keeps on.

DOMESTIC RABBIT (right) 'Whatever you do, please don't pick me up by my ears'. You should pick up a rabbit by the scruff of its neck and at the same time put your other hand underneath its rear as a support and carry it close to your body. This young butterfly English lop-eared rabbit is out for a bit of a run in the garden but he's not sure which way to go at the moment. It does make a change from living in a hutch to go for a bit of an amble around the garden. Of course you must have a rabbit that is used to being handled otherwise you may not be able to catch him.

Rabbits are very easy to keep providing you stick to a few simple rules. To start with you must give your rabbit a clean, dry hutch with a 'private' bedroom. You must be able to get at this and the main room to clean them out. It is best to be regular in your habits of feeding. The feed in the morning could be bran or oats and in the evening green stuff. Never offer wet leaves, just nice dry cabbage or lettuce or dandelion. Rabbits need water too and you can either put this in a dish or a bottle feeder. The great thing about all animals is that they must be kept clean and unless you are prepared to spend some time cleaning them it is perhaps better to forget about keeping pets. As well as cleaning out the hutch and putting in fresh hay or sawdust or fine peat, the rabbit, too needs a bit of a clean up. A small soft baby's brush is just the job and most rabbits will sit quietly and really enjoy a bit of hair-brushing.

INDEX

Sssssshhhhh, don't wake him up.
This baby chimpanzee (left) is
sound asleep. While he is sleeping
somewhere in Africa, the
bushbaby (above) is wide awake.
As you can see by his great big
eyes, he actually prefers to come
out at night.

ACKNOWLEDGEMENTS

The publishers wish to thank the following
organizations and individuals for their kind
permission to reproduce the photographs in
this book.

B & C Alexander 4-5, 67; Terry
Andrewarfha/Survival Anglia 41 inset; Animal
Graphics/Solitaire 76-77; Ardea (Valerie
Taylor) 25 below, (Donald Burgess) 47 inset,
(Hans Dossenbach) 50-51, (John Gooders)
52, (Ken Hoy) 58 below, (Peter Steyn) 80
right; B.B.C. Natural History Unit 6; Biofotos
32 below; S.C. Bisserot 56-57, 78; Fred
Bruemmer 24-25; Bruce Coleman Ltd. 22,
(Udo Hirsch) endpapers, (Fritz Prenzel) 16
left, (Norman Tomalin) 20-21, (Al Giddings)
26-27, (Donn Renn) 28-29, (Jack Dermid)
30-31, (Des Bartlett) 32 above left, Fritz
Vollmar 38-39, (K. Taylor) 61 inset, (Jane
Burton) 64-65, 72-73, 79, (Hans Reinhard)
68-69; Countryside Colour Library 34-35,
62-63; Bob Estall 66; Jeff Foott/Survival
Anglia 46-47, 54, 58-59; Robert Harding and
Associates 12-13, 14, 18, 36-37, 69 inset,
77 inset; Eric and David Hosking 44, 70-71;
Andrew Lazell 33 above; Jean Morris 15; Tony
and Marion Morrison 23, 26 inset; Natural
Science Photos (Ian Bennett) 8-9, (R.C.
Revels) 11; Dieter Plage/Survival Anglia 2-3;
Alan Root/Survival Anglia 16-17, 42-43, 45;
Satour 19, 55; Spectrum Colour Library
60-61, 80 left; Shin Yoshino 10, 48-49; Zefa
Picture Library 43 inset, 48 left,
(Rivers-Widaner) 1, (Hans Reinhard) 40-41,
74 left, (Bert Leidmann) 53, (F. Wolfsberger)
74-75.